CLIENT MANUAL

Overcoming Post-Traumatic Stress Disorder

■

A Cognitive-Behavioral
Exposure-Based Protocol
for the Treatment of PTSD
and the Other Anxiety Disorders

Larry Smyth, Ph.D.

Best Practices for Therapy
Empirically Based Treatment Protocols

Distributed in the U.S.A. by Publishers Group West; in Canada by Raincoast Books; in Great Britain by Airlift Book Company, Ltd.; in South Africa by Real Books, Ltd.; in Australia by Boobook; and in New Zealand by Tandem Press.

Copyright © 1999 by Larry Smyth, Ph.D.
New Harbinger Publications, Inc.
5674 Shattuck Avenue
Oakland, CA 94609

Cover design by Poulson\Gluck Design.
Edited by Donna Long.
Text design by Michele Waters.

Library of Congress Catalog Card Number: 98-67411
ISBN 1-57224-128-4 Paperback
`

New Harbinger Publications' Website address: www.newharbinger.com

01   00   99

10   9   8   7   6   5   4   3   2   1

First printing

Contents

About the Author

Larry Smyth received his doctorate degree in clinical psychology from Michigan State University in 1977. He is a Vietnam veteran and has been working with PTSD since 1982, when he began seeing combat-induced PTSD at Florida State University and in his private practice. He has been employed by the Department of Veteran Affairs since 1985 as a team leader, associate regional manager, and a regional manager for the Vet Center Program. Currently, he is a member of Trauma Services at the Baltimore Division of the Department of Veteran Affairs Maryland Health Care System. He also has a private practice and a courtesy staff appointment through Sheppard Pratt Hospital, where he specializes in the treatment of anxiety disorders on an outpatient basis. He can be reached at the following address:

Larry D. Smyth, Ph.D.
P. O. Box 642
Havre de Grace, MD 21078

Introduction

This manual is intended for individuals being treated for posttraumatic stress disorder (PTSD). It is also useful for the treatment of other anxiety disorders such as specific phobia, social phobia, panic disorder, generalized anxiety disorder, and obsessive-compulsive disorder. PTSD and other anxiety disorders can be effectively treated by way of the cognitive-behavioral exposure-based psychotherapy discussed in this book. Such treatment can be facilitated by medication, particularly SSRI antidepressants. The best approach is usually a combination of exposure-based psychotherapy and adjunctive medication, with the exact combination being determined by the individual and his or her therapist.

Well-informed clients do better in treatment than uninformed clients, so I ask that you read this entire manual, paying *particular* attention to the following sections: "What We Know about PTSD," "What We Know about Treating PTSD," "An Overview of the TAB-P Treatment Plan," "The Electrified Chair," "The Therapeutic Relationship," "Progress, Resistance, and Change," and "Traumatic Memory Work." At the beginning of each phase of treatment, review the sections specific to that phase. Be sure to discuss anything you don't understand with your therapist.

What Do We Know about Posttraumatic Stress Disorder?

Causes and Symptoms

The essential feature of posttraumatic stress disorder (PTSD) is an interlocking set of several anxiety disorders that develop as a consequence of an individual having been exposed to traumatic life-threatening events such as war, accidents, natural disasters, sexual assaults, and domestic violence. The PTSD sufferer usually experiences intense emotional distress upon recall of traumatic memories, and because of this distress the individual often tries to avoid the memories as well as people, objects, and situations that remind him or her of the traumatic experiences. Essentially, numerous phobias develop, the primary one being a phobia of memories. Efforts to avoid the traumatic memories are doomed to failure, however. They inevitably return in the form of nightmares and/or intrusive unwanted thoughts during the day. These reexperiencing symptoms occur because the traumatic memories are "stuck" in what is called the active memory system. The memories remain stuck and the reexperiencing symptoms persist until the anxiety or fear associated with the traumatic memories is reduced and the individual finds some way of making sense of the tragedy.

In addition to the phobias, the PTSD sufferer almost always worries about a repetition of the traumatic experiences and/or worries about losing emotional control and having an anxiety attack or a rage attack. This chronic worry, or generalized anxiety disorder, results in high levels of hyperarousal: the individual is constantly on edge, reacts with excessive irritability to daily annoyances, develops an exaggerated startle reflex, and often experiences impaired sleep. Sometimes such individuals develop panic disorder and come to fear bodily sensations such as chest pressure, feeling like they cannot breath, or dizziness. (These sensations are feared because they trigger either panic attacks or rage attacks.) In an effort to cope with these symptoms, many individuals begin to avoid people, places, and activities they previously enjoyed. This avoidance compounds the grief and depression related to their original traumatic experiences. Other individuals attempt to cope with their symptoms by drinking alcohol or using drugs, which temporarily reduces distress but actually worsens the symptoms over time and ultimately causes new problems. Many individuals experience a high level of emotional distress that significantly interferes with their relationships, health, and work. All too often, the individual's distress is compounded by the inability of some members of their social support group (neighbors, friends, coworkers, family members) to understand and fully appreciate the severity of the emotional distress. He or she is sometimes advised, "Just get over it. It's over and done with. Forget it and move on," or, "It's God's will." Although usually well-intentioned, such advice can alienate individuals from the people they need to help them recover.

Prevalence

Posttraumatic stress disorder is not uncommon. Approximately 75 percent of the adult population has experienced a life-threatening event at some point. Approximately 25 percent of those people develop PTSD as a consequence. Approximately 50 percent of the individuals who do develop it recover within two years without professional treatment. At any given time, about 6 percent of the adult population has full-blown or partial PTSD.

What Do We Know about Treating PTSD?

Exposure-based cognitive-behavioral therapy is the treatment of choice for PTSD. Compared to other types of psychotherapy, cognitive-behavioral therapy tends to have more scientific support and generally requires less time. Exposure-based cognitive-behavioral therapy is a specialized set of strategies that research has shown to be very effective with anxiety disorders in general and PTSD in particular. Both prolonged-exposure strategies and brief-exposure strategies have been found to be effective. Exposure strategies are simply ways of helping clients approach their traumatic memories and approach people, places, or things that are associated with their traumatic memories in a manner that is not too overwhelming. Cognitive-behavioral therapy that employs only brief-exposure strategies appears to have higher relapse rates than therapy that employs only prolonged-exposure strategies, however. (Relapses occur when symptoms that were eliminated in the course of treatment return after treatment has ended.) On the other hand, cognitive-behavioral therapy that employs only prolonged-exposure strategies appears to result in more adverse treatment outcomes than therapy that employs only brief-exposure strategies. (Adverse treatment outcomes refer to such things as clients dropping out of treatment before it is completed, or experiencing unwanted side effects.) Combining brief-exposure and prolonged-exposure strategies in the same treatment protocol seems to be more effective than using only one or the other.

Approximately 75 percent of those who seek out treatment recover in fifteen sessions or less, provided they receive cognitive-behavioral exposure-based psychotherapy. Adjunctive medication, particularly antidepressants such as Prozac, Paxil, Elavil, or Zoloft, can also be quite helpful. These medications not only help with depression but can also help with sleep disturbances, generalized anxiety, and panic attacks. Minor tranquilizers such as Ativan, Buspar, or Xanax are sometimes helpful as well, particularly with hyperarousal symptoms. Caution should always be exercised with the minor tranquilizers because of their potential for abuse, however. The correct combination of psychotherapy and medication is usually best determined on an individual basis. Not all PTSD can be treated so quickly and effectively, however. For example, PTSD that is complicated by a chronic substance-abuse disorder usually takes longer to treat, as does PTSD produced by multiple traumatic experiences that occur over an extensive period of time, such as prisoner-of-war experiences or prolonged domestic violence. Nonetheless, complex PTSD, or PTSD complicated by other disorders, can be effectively treated with cognitive-behavioral exposure-based psychotherapy and medication—it just takes somewhat longer.

An Overview of the TAB-P Treatment Plan

The TAB-P protocol, an exposure-based approach, emphasizes the importance of the therapeutic relationship (T), assimilation strategies (A), and integrating brief-exposure strategies (B) with prolonged-exposure strategies (P). This is a gentle form of psychotherapy. Clients are never asked to confront distress-inducing memories, worries, sensations, objects, or situations in such a manner or at such a pace as to provoke overwhelmingly intense levels of emotional distress. Some distress is inevitable, of course, but it is always in the mild to moderate range. The essential elements that make up the six phases and fifteen sessions of the TAB-P protocol are described below.

- Phase I (assessment and goal setting): sessions 1 and 2
  In this phase, your therapist will conduct a thorough evaluation of your particular situation so that he or she can tailor the therapy to your particular needs. A positive, supportive, and collaborative relationship should be forged with your therapist in the process. Normally, this takes one or two sessions. The evaluation usually involves your answering a series of questions and possibly completing some questionnaires pertaining to physical health, medication, relationships, previous treatment, mental health, and so on. The goals that are set will depend on the complexity of your PTSD as well as on such practical matters as your motivation for treatment, the amount of time you have available for treatment, and your willingness to complete homework assignments. If your PTSD is uncomplicated, complete elimination of all of your symptoms within fifteen sessions of therapy can and should be expected. If you have complex PTSD or your PTSD is complicated by other disorders, complete elimination of your symptoms may not be feasible. Instead, a marked reduction in the severity, frequency, or vexatiousness of your symptoms might be more realistic.

- Phase II (emotion-focused coping-skills training): sessions 3 and 4
  In this phase, you will be trained to use two emotion-focused coping skills, the eye-movement technique and the relaxation response, to control your distress when you're conducting exposure work. Normally, this takes two sessions.

- Phase III (assimilation work): session 5
  In this phase, you will be trained in assimilation and rational thinking, another set of emotion-focused coping skills. You will also begin reviewing your traumatic memories using this set of skills. Initially this will be done in sessions with your therapist, but later it will be done on your own with tape recordings of your therapy sessions. With repeated reviews, the distress will subside. This phase may last between one and nine sessions. Should assimilation and rational thinking prove insufficient to manage your distress during the reviews, this phase will be terminated and you will proceed to the brief-exposure phase.

- Phase IV (brief exposure and assimilation work): sessions 6 to 11
  In this phase you will begin applying the emotion-focused coping skills you learned in previous phases, which will help you control your distress while you briefly expose yourself (in your imagination) to traumatic memories and other trauma-related cues such as thoughts, worries, images, objects, sensations, or situations. Once you have repeatedly demonstrated that you can control your distress when briefly exposed to these cues in your imagination, you will progress to briefly exposing yourself to these same distress-producing cues in real-life settings. Once strong coping skills have developed by way of the real-life brief-exposure exercises, you will progress to the prolonged-exposure work phase. Occasionally the brief-exposure work phase can be omitted and an individual can proceed directly to the prolonged-exposure work phase. This tends to shorten the duration of treatment, but unwanted side effects can sometimes develop. Four sessions are normally required for this phase of treatment.

- Phase V (prolonged exposure and assimilation work): sessions 12 and 13
  In this phase, you will again apply the emotion-focused coping skills you learned in previous phases, but you will apply them while reviewing your distress-producing memories, worries, thoughts, images, sensations, objects, and situations for prolonged periods of time. These exposure exercises will first be conducted in imagination and then later in real life. Prolonged-exposure work emphasizes the use of assimilation and rational-thinking strategies to manage the distress generated by the prolonged exposure, hastening the development of desensitization effects. Desensitization effects are defined as a reduction in the distress experienced when confronting distress-producing cues after one or more exposure trials. This reduction is experienced as occurring outside of the individual's control: "It just doesn't upset me like it used to." Brief-exposure work, on the other hand, hastens the development of coping effects. Coping effects are defined as an increase in the ease, quickness, and confidence with which individuals can calm themselves down when confronting distress-producing cues. This reduction is experienced as under the individual's control: "It still bothers me a lot, but I know I won't lose it. I can stop those panic and rage attacks. I know I can control my distress by using the eye-movement technique, the relaxation response, and rational thinking." Prolonged-exposure work normally takes two to three sessions, provided sufficient brief-exposure work has preceded it.

- Phase VI (relapse prevention work): sessions 14 and 15
  You will come back to see your therapist once or twice after completing your treatment. During these follow-up sessions, your therapist will review how you have been doing with respect to your PTSD symptoms, and will inquire about your life and mental health in general. He or she will also discuss ways of insuring that the gains you have made are maintained. Should the symptoms return or any unmanageable problems arise, some additional treatment may be in order.

Goals and Duration of Treatment

Establishing realistic treatment goals at the outset of treatment is very important in the TAB-P protocol and other cognitive-behavioral exposure-based psychotherapies. The goals will vary from person to person depending on the complexity of the PTSD as well as on such practical matters as motivation for treatment, willingness to complete homework assignments, and the amount of time available for treatment. In many cases of uncomplicated PTSD of recent origin, complete elimination of all PTSD symptoms within fifteen sessions can and should be expected. In other cases, complete elimination of the person's PTSD symptoms may not be realistic. Instead, reducing the PTSD symptoms to the point that they no longer significantly interfere with your life might be more feasible. Or, a realistic treatment goal might be simply to restore you to a level of functioning that existed prior to an intensification of the PTSD symptoms brought about by substance abuse, marital problems, or a financial crisis. In the case of particularly long-standing PTSD produced by multiple traumatic experiences, a realistic treatment goal might be to keep you from getting any worse by helping you problem-solve situational stressors and reduce your social isolation. Whatever your particular treatment goals turn out to be, it is important that both you and your therapist agree on them. This agreement should include what to expect in terms of your PTSD symptoms as well as agreement as to the number of sessions required and the treatment strategies to be used.

Self-Rating Scales

I recommend assessing your progress at the outset of each session. This can be done in a relatively straightforward fashion by simply informing your therapist of the number of target symptoms you had in the past week. For example, "I had five nightmares this week, each generating six to eight SUDs, and it took me over three hours to return to sleep each time I had one." (You'll learn about SUDs below and throughout your treatment.) Assessment can also be accomplished by more formal instruments such as the Brief Symptom Inventory or the PTSD Self-Assessment Questionnaire, which each take only about five minutes to complete. (The Questionnaire is printed below, following the SUD scale; if you're interested in the Brief Inventory, ask your therapist about it.) Finally, another valuable scale is the SUD scale, which stands for "subjective units of distress." The SUD scale enables you to quickly communicate the intensity of your distress, which is very important during exposure work. Also, I recommend completing the Modified PTSD Symptom Scale now (at the beginning of treatment) and just before ending treatment, you'll find it immediately following the PTSD Self Assessment Questionnaire.

Homework Assignments and Agenda Setting

Homework will be very important during the course of your treatment, because successfully completed homework assignments greatly reduce the number of therapy sessions required to treat PTSD and the other anxiety disorders. Initial assignments involve practicing the emotion-focused coping skills you will be taught. Later, your assignments will involve applying these emotion-focused coping skills when confronting your traumatic memories and other feared objects in imaginal exposure work and in real life. All homework assignments will be negotiated, meaning that your therapist will make sure you are in agreement and have the resources necessary to do them. Should you not complete an agreed-upon assignment, your therapist will explore the reasons for this with you. Hopefully, a solution can be found so that future homework assignments are completed as negotiated.

Setting an agenda near the beginning of each session is also very important in the TAB-P protocol, as well as in cognitive-behavioral psychotherapy in general. The agendas should be determined by the results of your previous session and by your most recent homework assignment. Agendas keep both you and your therapist on track and increase the likelihood that you will reach your treatment goals in the agreed-upon number of sessions.

Subjective Units of Distress (SUD) Scale

The subjective units of distress—or SUD—scale is a convenient way of communicating to other people how much distress you are experiencing at any given time. There are eleven points on the scale, ranging from zero (absolutely complete relaxation) up to ten (extreme distress). Please review this scale and have the ratings fixed in your mind so that when your therapist asks you for a "SUD rating" you can quickly communicate to him or her your level of distress.

Rating

Zero: Complete relaxation. Deep sleep; no distress at all.

One: Awake but very relaxed; dosing off. Your mind wanders and drifts, similar to what you might feel just prior to falling asleep.

Two: Relaxing at the beach, relaxing at home in front of a warm fire on a wintry day, or walking peacefully in the woods.

Three: The amount of tension and stress needed to keep your attention from wandering, to keep your head erect, and so on. This tension and stress is not experienced as unpleasant; it is "normal."

Four: Mild distress such as mild feelings of bodily tension, mild worry, mild apprehension, mild fear, or mild anxiety. Somewhat unpleasant but easily tolerated.

Five: Mild to moderate distress. Distinctly unpleasant but insufficient to produce many bodily symptoms.

Six: Moderate distress. Very unpleasant feelings of fear, anxiety, anger, worry, apprehension, and/or substantial bodily tension such as a headache or upset stomach. Distinctly unpleasant but tolerable sensations; you're still able to think clearly. What most people would describe as a "bad day," but your ability to work, drive, converse, and so on is not impeded.

Seven: Moderately high distress that makes concentration hard. Fairly intense bodily distress.

Eight: High distress. High levels of fear, anxiety, worry, apprehension, and/or bodily tension. These feelings cannot be tolerated very long. Thinking and problem-solving is impaired. Bodily distress is substantial. To work, drive, converse, and so on is difficult.

Nine: High to extreme distress. Thinking is substantially impaired.

Ten: Extreme distress, panic- and terror-stricken, extreme bodily tension. The maximum amount of fear, anxiety, and/or apprehension you can possibly imagine.

PTSD Self-Assessment Questionnaire

Name: _____

Date: _____

Please rate the frequency of your symptoms in the past week (or other time period specified by your therapist). Use the SUD scale to rate the average amount of distress you experienced for each symptom.

	Frequency	Average SUDs
1. Number of nightmares in which you relived a traumatic event:		
2. Number of intrusive unwanted thoughts during the day about a traumatic event:		
3. Number of panic attacks:		
4. Number of times you avoided a situation, person, or an activity out of fear of a panic attack, an intrusive thought, or loss of control of your anger:		

Modified PTSD Symptom Scale

Developed by Sherry Falsetti, Heidi Resnick, Patricia Resick & Dean Kilpatrick
Medical University of South Carolina & University of Missouri—St. Louis

Instructions: The purpose of this scale is to measure the frequency and severity of symptoms in <u>the past two weeks</u>. Using the scale below, please indicate the frequency of symptoms to the left of each item. Then indicate the severity beside each item by circling the letter that fits you best.

FREQUENCY

0 = Not at all

1 = Once per week or less/a little bit/
    once in a while

2 = 2 to 4 times per week/somewhat/
    half the time

3 = 5 or more times per week/very much/
    almost

SEVERITY

A = Not at all distressing

B = A little bit distressing

C = Moderately distressing

D = Quite a bit distressing

E = Extremely distressing

FREQUENCY | SEVERITY

_____ 1. Have you had recurrent or intrusive distressing thoughts or recollections about the event(s)?   A B C D E

_____ 2. Have you been having recurrent bad dreams or nightmares about the event(s)?   A B C D E

_____ 3. Have you had the experience of suddenly reliving the event(s), flashbacks of it, acting or feeling as if it were re-occurring?   A B C D E

_____ 4. Have you been intensely emotionally upset when reminded of the event(s) (includes anniversary reactions)?   A B C D E

_____ 5. Have you persistently been making efforts to avoid thoughts or feelings associated with the event(s) we've talked about?   A B C D E

_____ 6. Have you persistently been making efforts to avoid activities, situations, or places that remind you of the event(s)?   A B C D E

_____ 7. Are there any important aspects about the event(s) that you still cannot recall?   A B C D E

_____ 8. Have you markedly lost interest in free time activities since the event(s)?   A B C D E

FREQUENCY

0 = Not at all

1 = Once per week or less/a little bit/ once in a while

2 = 2 to 4 times per week/somewhat/ half the time

3 = 5 or more times per week/very much/almost always

SEVERITY

A = Not at all distressing

B = A little bit distressing

C = Moderately distressing

D = Quite a bit distressing

E = Extremely distressing

FREQUENCY

SEVERITY

_____	9. Have you felt detached or cut off from others around you since the event(s)?	A B C D E
_____	10. Have you felt that your ability to experience emotions is less (e.g., unable to have loving feelings, feeling numb, can't cry when sad, etc.)?	A B C D E
_____	11. Have you felt that any future plans or hopes have changed because of the event(s) (e.g., no career, marriage, children, or long life)?	A B C D E
_____	12. Have you been having persistent difficulty falling or staying asleep?	A B C D E
_____	13. Have you been continuously irritable or having anger outbursts?	A B C D E
_____	14. Have you been having persistent difficulty concentrating?	A B C D E
_____	15. Are you overly alert (e.g., check to see who is around you) since the event(s)?	A B C D E
_____	16. Have you been jumpier, more easily startled, since the event(s)?	A B C D E
_____	17. Have you been having intense PHYSICAL REACTIONS (e.g., sweaty, heart palpitations) when reminded of the event(s)?	A B C D E

Assessment and Goal Setting

Sessions 1 and 2

Goals:

- Establish a good working relationship with your therapist.

- Decide upon your treatment goals.

- Learn about cognitive-behavioral therapy.

- Learn about PTSD and other anxiety disorders.

- Assess your problems.

- Define your treatment goals.

- Negotiate homework assignments. Probable homework assignment for this phase:

Complete a self-assessment to get an idea of how you are doing overall.

There are two primary objectives to be accomplished in this phase: develop a good working relationship with your therapist and establish realistic treatment goals. Establishing realistic treatment goals includes coming to an agreement with your therapist as to what you expect to accomplish, such as eliminating your nightmares and panic attacks. It also includes deciding upon the treatment strategies, as well as the number of sessions likely required to reach your goals. To accomplish this, your therapist will ask you a number of questions to clarify the nature of your problems and will probably ask you to complete a few questionnaires. Usually this process takes no more than two sessions.

The Electrified Chair: How Irrational Anxiety Develops and How to Treat It

What is Irrational Anxiety?

Irrational anxiety is nothing more than excessive anxiety or fear that is experienced in situations that are not really dangerous. For example, a person with an irrational fear of dogs knows that a small, docile dog is not really dangerous. Nonetheless, he or she may well experience high levels of fear while in a room with such a dog. The fear is irrational or out of proportion to the actual dangerousness of the situation. Irrational anxiety is a very important concept because it plays a major role in all the anxiety disorders.

Is Irrational Anxiety the Same as a Phobia?

Irrational anxiety and fear are sometimes called phobias, particularly when the person experiencing it attempts to manage them through avoidance. People can develop irrational fears or phobias of all kinds of things: dogs, elevators, and activities such as giving a speech (referred to as a social phobia). They can also develop irrational fears of their memories (posttraumatic stress disorder) and unusual bodily sensations such as dizziness (panic disorder).

What Causes "Irrational" Anxiety or Phobias?

Perhaps the best way to understand "irrational" anxiety is to use the fanciful notion of an electrified chair to explain how this anxiety can develop as well as explain the related concepts of conditioned anxiety and the generalization of anxiety. Suppose, for a moment, that your chair has been wired in such a way that every time you sat in it you received an electric shock. Suppose you had sat in this chair one time and had received a very painful shock. What do you suppose you would think when you approached this chair the second time after receiving this very painful shock? Probably something to the effect of, "Oh, no! I'm going to get another one of those terrible shocks from that chair! It's going to hurt a lot! Maybe it will kill me!" And what do you suppose you would feel as you approached the chair and said these things to yourself? Yes, you would probably feel quite anxious and fearful. That is, your actual experience of being shocked by the chair coupled with your thoughts and expectations, or what you say to yourself as you approach the chair, both strongly contribute to how much anxiety or fear you experience in the presence of the electrified chair. Now suppose that you have sat in the chair a hundred times and have received a painful shock each and every time. What do you suppose you would be thinking or saying to yourself as you approached the electrified chair now? Well, you would probably be saying pretty much the same thing you were saying to yourself when you approached the chair the second time, but you would likely be saying it in a shorthand fashion. For example, you might only say, "Uh, oh" to yourself, but "Uh, oh" would have the same meaning to you as the longer phrases you were uttering to yourself the first few times you approached the chair. The abbreviated, shorthand messages are called automatic thoughts. What are you feeling at this time? Again, you would probably feel quite anxious and fearful not only because of your painful experiences with the chair but also because of your automatic thoughts. This type of anxiety is called conditioned anxiety.

Now, what do you suppose would happen if you approached other chairs in the room after receiving a hundred shocks in the chair and pairing these shocks with your automatic thoughts? Yes, even though you had never received any shocks in these other unwired chairs you would probably experience a considerable amount of anxiety or fear as you approached them. This process is called the generalization of anxiety, and automatic thoughts play a big part in this process just as they do in conditioned anxiety. That is, if you think to yourself something such as, "These other chairs are just like the electrified chair" as you approach them, you are going to experience what is called irrational anxiety. It is highly likely that this self-talk is going to occur in the form of highly condensed, brief automatic thoughts such as, "Uh, oh." And because this self-talk is so condensed, brief, and automatic, it is also highly likely that you will not be consciously aware of your automatic thoughts when they occur. Thus, you can become irrationally afraid of many things that have never actually harmed you. The key to this process is automatic thoughts.

To illustrate this using another example, suppose the chair in which you received all those shocks was unplugged and you knew it was impossible for you to receive another shock. What do you suppose you would feel as you approached this chair after receiving a hundred shocks from it, knowing full well that it was no longer dangerous as you could see it was unplugged? Yes, despite knowing that the chair was no longer dangerous, you would likely experience considerable anxiety or fear anyway—your anxiety or fear of the chair would now be irrational. And again, what would be causing this fear? Yes, automatic thoughts such as "Uh, oh" would likely occur as you approached the unplugged chair, and these thoughts would result in you being irrationally afraid of the chair even though you knew it was no longer dangerous.

Once a Phobia Has Developed, Can Anything Else Go Wrong?

Yes, it can and frequently does. Suppose, for instance, that you had developed some conditioned anxiety to the electrified chair, and the conditioned anxiety had generalized to other chairs by way of automatic thoughts so that now you irrationally feared all kinds of chairs and attempted to manage your anxiety by avoiding chairs all together. What do you imagine you might come to think about yourself and your world under these circumstances? Perhaps you would come to think of yourself as stupid, weak, or crazy for having such a fear, and your efforts to avoid chairs probably would greatly interfere with work, friends, family, and fun, causing you to miss out on many of the pleasant things life has to offer. You might also come to think of your future as hopeless and yourself as worthless and helpless. How do you suppose you would feel if you thought hopeless, worthless, and helpless thoughts most of the time? You would likely become depressed in addition to having a phobia. Suppose that instead of such thoughts you constantly reflected on the injustice or the unfairness of having a phobia of chairs. How do you suppose you would feel then? Probably very angry much of the time. Suppose that instead of those thoughts you frequently thought about the possibility of yourself losing control of your anger or your anxiety in the presence of other people and concluded that you would be humiliated or gravely endangered if this occurred? And what if you attempted to cope with this fear of humiliation and/or fear of violence by avoiding virtually all people? Yes, your anxiety would probably become much worse and you would probably feel depressed as well. So as you can see, sometimes feelings of depression or anger can develop as a consequence of a phobia, and sometimes additional fears can develop as well.

How Do You Treat Irrational Fears or Phobias?

Suppose you had developed a phobia of the electrified chair by way of conditioned anxiety and your fear had generalized by way of automatic thoughts to chairs of all types. Suppose you decided it was high time to rid yourself of this fear since your avoidance of chairs was seriously interfering with your work and with your family. How might you go about teaching yourself that chairs aren't dangerous? By approaching chairs rather than avoiding them you would find that your fear would gradually subside—provided, of course, that you didn't receive any more shocks. This process of repetitively approaching the feared object is called exposure work. There are two basic ways of conducting exposure work. One way would be to choose a chair to approach and then force yourself to sit in it for an hour or two. Initially, you would experience very intense anxiety but by the end of an hour or two your anxiety would have subsided and your self-talk would have changed from "Uh, oh!" (which meant you perceived yourself to be in grave danger of receiving a very painful shock) to something like, "I don't particularly like this chair, but it's not dangerous; it can't hurt me. I'm safe." This type of exposure work, in which you reduce your irrational anxiety by approaching the feared object for a lengthy period of time, is called prolonged-exposure work.

Another way you could reduce your irrational anxiety would be to gradually approach chairs for brief periods of time. For example, you might approach to within about ten feet of a chair and remain there until your anxiety had subsided and your self-talk had changed to something such as, "At least at ten feet, chairs are not dangerous. I can handle it." Then, you might approach to within about one foot of a chair and remain at this distance until your anxiety had subsided and your automatic thinking had changed. Next, you might briefly touch a chair repetitively for a second or two until your anxiety had subsided and your automatic thinking had changed. Next, you might briefly sit in a chair repetitively, and so on. This type of exposure work, in which you more gradually reduce your automatic thought-mediated irrational anxiety by approaching the feared object for relatively brief periods of time, is called brief-exposure work.

Is Prolonged-Exposure Work Better Than Brief-Exposure Work at Reducing Irrational Anxiety?

Yes and no. Prolonged-exposure work is more efficient and quicker than brief-exposure work at reducing excessive irrational anxiety. However, prolonged-exposure work generally creates high levels of distress at the outset of treatment, which some people are unwilling or unable to tolerate. Thus, it is often a very good idea to begin reducing irrational anxiety by starting with brief-exposure work and then moving on to prolonged-exposure work once your tolerance for exposure work has been enhanced and you have the confidence to proceed.

Is Exposure Work Always Done in the Real World?

No. Sometimes exposure work is conducted by imagining feared situations, feared things, feared memories, and so on before actually approaching these feared objects in real life. This is called imaginal-exposure work and it can be done in the form of either prolonged-exposure work or brief-exposure work. Using the chair phobia as an example, a person might be asked to vividly imagine himself approaching and sitting in chairs until his irrational anxiety subsides and his automatic thoughts are changed before asking him to approach chairs in real life. When approaching chairs in real life, the person is said to be conducting in vivo exposure work ("in vivo" means "in real life"). Generally speaking, it is often beneficial to conduct imaginal-exposure work prior to conducting in vivo exposure work.

Is Exposure Work All That Is Needed to Reduce Irrational Anxiety?

Sometimes exposure work is all that is needed, particularly when the irrational anxiety is in the form of specific phobias, that is, limited to very specific situations (such as public speaking) or to very specific objects (such as dogs) and has not generalized very much. Sometimes, however, the exposure work must be accompanied by efforts to reduce excessive emotional distress in the form of depression, guilt or shame, and/or anger that can develop along with or because of the irrational fear, such as is often seen in posttraumatic stress disorder. Efforts to reduce these other emotional reactions usually requires that the therapist help the individuals change their beliefs and self-talk with regard to themselves and their world in addition to changing their beliefs and self-talk about the object that provokes their irrational anxiety.

The Therapeutic Relationship in Cognitive-Behavioral Therapy

What Type of Relationship Should I Establish with My Therapist?

Probably the best type of relationship is a student-teacher or an athlete-coach, with you in the role of an athlete or student and your therapist in the role of a coach or teacher.

What Responsibilities Do I Have?

First, hire the therapist as your coach and allow him or her to actually coach you. In one way or another, you are saying, "I'm not running the race of life fast enough," or "I'm not jumping the hurdles well enough for my satisfaction, and I want you to help me improve my game." Second, you need to establish realistic goals for yourself. You may not be able to run a four-minute mile, but with training and the proper coaching, you may well be able to run an eight-minute mile—a substantial improvement over the twelve-minute mile you are currently running. You may also learn to effectively jump the obstacles placed in your path, rather than trip over them. Third, you have to train on your own between coaching sessions. The therapist-coach will show you a variety of ways to improve your game during the coaching sessions, but you will have to practice them on your own, outside the coaching sessions, before they will do you much good. Fourth, you will have to actually enter some races, because there's no way to win one otherwise. Fifth, learn from your mistakes rather than berate yourself for making them.

What Responsibilities Does My Therapist Have?

First, your therapist-coach will assist you in setting realistic goals. Second, he or she will teach you some skills for running the race of life better. Third, your therapist-coach will encourage you to try out these new skills, and he or she will help you pace yourself in applying your newly acquired skills. Your therapist-coach may get firm and directive with you, if he or she senses you are not practicing between coaching sessions or are unwilling to enter any races. Remember, your therapist-coach is concerned with you, as well as with your task of running the race of life better. He or she cannot run the race for you, however.

Can the Therapist-Coach Cure Me?

Absolutely not. Counseling in general, and cognitive-behavioral therapy in particular, is not psychosurgery wherein the therapist operates on a passive patient to remove a diseased part. Learning to run the race better depends primarily on how hard you work. Good coaching can help, but it is still largely up to you.

Progress, Resistance, and Change in Cognitive-Behavioral Therapy

Will I Always Make Steady Progress?

No, probably not. Steady progress toward the reduction or elimination of excessive distress is the exception rather than the rule. In most cases, periods of gains will alternate with periods of no obvious gains. Occasionally distress intensifies, but these periods are normally brief. Do not get discouraged if you hit a period of no progress. Remember, two steps forward and one step back is normal when overcoming chronic and excessive distress.

Is It Possible I Will Resist Getting Better?

Perhaps. As strange as it may seem, people sometimes do resist reducing their distress and getting better. There are a number of reasons for this. Sometimes symptoms become part of a person's self-identity, and to be without them would be like walking down the street half-naked. For example, imagine a person born with a crippled leg who suddenly grew a new perfect leg. Although the new leg may have been something he very much wanted, he had been crippled for twenty-five years and had come to think of himself as crippled. With his new leg, he must think of himself in an entirely different light. And he, as well as others, might come to expect new and different things of him. "Am I able to meet these expectations and challenges, and do I really want to?" are questions he might pose to himself. The resulting uncertainty and possibility of failure could generate anxiety and a desire to hang on to the crippled leg. It is not always easy to change from victim to survivor, nor is it easy to change from crippled child to functional adult. Change, even for the better, can be stressful, and resistance sometimes occurs in the process. You should not be dismayed if it does occur. Instead, recognize resistance for what it is, and work with your therapist to find ways of getting over, around, or through it. Probably the most common ways of resisting getting better are missing appointments and failing to complete homework assignments. Other ways include showing up late for appointments and delaying getting to work during the treatment sessions.

Money you receive for your illness could also cause some resistance. If you are receiving or expect to receive money for being disabled as a result of anxiety or stress, it is extremely important that you discuss the matter truthfully with your therapist. Hopefully, arrangements can be made so that getting better will have little or no bearing on whether or not you are paid for your distress.

Occasionally, other people in your life could resist your efforts to get better. As people move from being a victim or crippled child to being a survivor and a functional adult, resentment and sabotage by family members and friends are sometimes encountered. These forms of resistance usually stem from uncertainty about whether the "new you" will still need or want them. It is also possible the "new you" will require changes in them that they may not want to make. For instance, suppose a crippled man recovers from his disability and begins assuming more and more responsibility for parenting his children and managing the family finances. He may find his wife resenting his recovery and being unwilling to relinquish some of her parental and financial power. Although resistance sometimes does occur in the process of getting better, it is important to not get into the blame game. Instead, simply recognize resistance for what it is, and, again, work with your therapist to find ways of getting over, around, or through it.

Will I Have to Do Anything More, Once I Have Learned to Control My Distress and Have Eliminated Most of My Symptoms?

Possibly. Sometimes people learn to control their distress, or even eliminate their psychological symptoms, yet find themselves behaving in the same manner they did when they were overwhelmed with distress. For example, suppose a man finds himself staying at home and remaining socially isolated even though his panic attacks have stopped. In such a case, he may have to force himself to try out new behaviors, new situations, and new roles. It may take some time before he will feel comfortable in these new pursuits, and he probably will find some of them to his liking (and others not). What is important is that he try them out, because there is no way to tell which activities he will like and which he won't without actually attempting them.

Traumatic Memory Work in the Treatment of Posttraumatic Stress Disorder

What Is the Purpose of Traumatic-Memory Work?

The purpose of traumatic-memory work is to change memories of traumatic life events from "hot" memories to "bad" memories. Hot memories are defined as memories of traumatic events that occurred in the past and that, upon recall, elicit moderate to intense distress experienced as high levels of anxiety, fear, grief, guilt, shame, anger, and/or depression. Bad memories, on the other hand, are defined as memories of traumatic events that occurred in the past and that, upon recall, elicit unpleasant but tolerable distress in the mild to moderate range.

What Makes Hot Memories Hot?

Memories are hot because the traumatic life event threatened the individual who experienced it in at least one of four ways. The event threatened the life or physical well-being of the individual or other people (life threat), it threatened beliefs or expectations that the individual held about himself or herself and valued highly (self-ideal threat), it threatened assumptions or expectations about the world and the people in it that the person highly valued (worldview threat), and/or the memory arouses impulses (usually aggressive) that the individual believes will be severely punished by society if they are acted upon (impulse threat). In most cases, the memories are threatening because of a combination of life threat and one or more of the other three types of threats.

What Is Meant by Life Threat?

Life threat simply refers to a serious threat to someone's life or limbs or physical harm or loss of life that actually took place. High levels of fear or anxiety would be considered normal emotional reactions to this type of threat.

What Is Meant by Self-Ideal Threat?

We all have conceptions of our psychological selves, for example, one might consider oneself to be very honest, trustworthy, compassionate, intelligent, courageous, competent, or loyal, with some of these traits more highly valued than others. Sometimes traumatic life events cause us to think, feel, or behave in ways that contradict our sense of self, and when our highly valued traits are contradicted, intense distress usually results. For instance, an individual might consider himself (or herself) to be a very compassionate person and highly value that trait in himself, but later he might find himself becoming calloused and indifferent to human suffering after being hardened by combat. The memory of his indifference then could prove to be hot because the memory threatens a highly valued part of himself.

What Is Meant by Worldview Threat?

We all have conceptions, assumptions, or beliefs about our world and the people who populate it that help us understand and predict what has and will occur. These expectations help us make sense of the world. Examples of such assumptions are: "There is a just and loving God," "It is a just world," "Good things happen to good people," "If you work hard you will always be rewarded," "Justice will always prevail in the end," "People are good and trustworthy," "Leaders are good, competent individuals who earned their positions and look out for their people," "It's a safe world," "It's a predictable world," "People are basically good," and "I'm good."

Sometimes traumatic life events present us with information that contradicts some of our most cherished assumptions about the world. For instance, the death of a young child may contradict assumptions about a just world or a just and loving God. The memory of this child's death could prove to be hot because it shatters highly valued assumptions or expectations that the person had about the rules governing their world. The result would be high levels of distress upon recall of the memory.

What Is Meant by Impulse Threat?

Sometimes traumatic life events arouse very strong impulses or wishes, such as strong feelings of anger or rage and intense wishes to retaliate aggressively against others. The individual may then, in turn, fear that he or she will lose control of these aggressive wishes and actually harm someone. The person may feel overwhelming guilt for having these wishes. Memories of the traumatic event become hot because the memory itself comes to elicit these dangerously aggressive wishes or impulses.

Why Don't Hot Memories and the Emotions Associated with Them Fade with Time?

Actually, many traumatic memories and the intense emotions associated with them do fade over time, but not always. The most common reason for this is that the memory is not translated into words and expressed to supportive others such as friends, parents, or spouses in a safe environment. The second most common reason is that the natural curative power of dreaming about traumatic events is hindered by drugs or alcohol, and/or the emotions associated with the memory are so intense that they constantly awaken the individual from his or her sleep before the natural desensitization process of dreaming can occur. The third most common reason is that the individual does not have any self-ideals or worldviews that could make sense of the trauma and replace the old self-ideals or worldviews that were shattered by the traumatic event. Consequently, the memory doesn't make any sense, cannot be assimilated, and therefore cannot be relegated to long-term memory. Instead, it is stored in intermediate memory (active memory) only to repeatedly return to conscious awareness in the form of intrusive thoughts during the day and nightmares at night. The information contained in the traumatic memories is simply too important and too contradictory to the individual's view of himself or to his view of the world to be forgotten. In short, there are lessons to be learned, and the mind will not allow the memory to be transferred into long-term memory or be forgotten until those lessons are understood and the prevailing schemas/assumptions about one's self and one's world have been altered in such a way as to accommodate (make sense of) the discordant information contained in the traumatic memory.

An Exercise in Traumatic-Memory Work

As you read the description of the trauma below, try to determine what type of threats are being posed by the memory of this trauma. Speculate about how these threats might be resolved, or worked through, in order to transform the memory from a hot memory into a bad memory.

A young child is terminally ill with cancer and is on his deathbed. It has been a prolonged and agonizing death; the parents have known he was terminally ill for six months, and now the child is racked with pain as the cancer has invaded his central nervous system, causing convulsions every minute or two. The convulsions prohibit the child from breathing, so he is suffocating along with being racked with pain. The father begs the physician in attendance to give his son a lethal dose of the pain medication that the physician is injecting, but the physician refuses. The father then attempts to kill his son by suffocating him with a pillow. The child finally succumbs to a heart attack.

Threats:

1. Life threat. The father's son died and he became acutely aware of his own mortality and the mortality of the rest of his family. "Disease and accidents don't just happen to the other guy. They happened to me and they could happen again."

2. Self-ideal threat. The father loved his son and always thought of himself as a good father. In this instance, he felt that being a good father required that he kill his own son to spare him the agony, but "You don't kill people, let alone your own son." Killing him would be regarded as murder since euthanasia was illegal in the state in which he lived. The father also thought about the possibility of the police and courts becoming involved if he did kill his son, and he felt that his wife and other children had gone through enough already: "They didn't need any more pain."

3. Worldview threats. The father had a number of core beliefs or assumptions that were challenged by the trauma, including: there is a just and loving God, it is a safe world, it is a just world, it is a predictable and orderly world, and people in authority can be trusted to do the right thing.

4. Impulse threat. The father experienced intense rage following the death of his son, threatening his sense of self.

Resolutions:

Resolution of the life threat was resolved by the passage of time in the absence of any more serious threats to the father's loved ones. At first, he felt extremely vulnerable; every sniffle of his remaining child was viewed with great alarm. He found it difficult to read newspapers or watch television because of the pervasiveness of the tragedies they depict. Gradually, however, his *healthy* denial returned as he constantly reminded himself, "Sometimes life can be very dangerous, as it was for my son, but there is every reason to believe my daughter is healthy and will remain so. I can't continue to be overprotective; this isn't good for her or me. Of course, it is possible that more harm can come to my family, but it is unlikely. The best I can do is be reasonably cautious about things I can control, such as my driving. It doesn't do any good to worry about things like leukemia, over which I have no control. It's best to sort of pretend these things don't exist, since I can't do anything about them."

The self-ideal threat was resolved by getting the father to stop asking the question, "Did I make the right decision?" Instead, he was encouraged to ask the question, "Did I make a reasonable decision under the circumstances?" Implicit in the first question was the assumption that good, competent people always make the right decisions. This assumption had to be modified to allow for the fact that sometimes life presents us with damned-if-you-do-and-damned-if-you-don't situations in which there are no right answers, just several wrong ones to choose from. People certainly do not like it when they're presented with such situations, but we all encounter them from time to time. In this instance, the father had the choice of either killing his son or not killing his son, and regardless of what he decided, he was going to be making a bad decision with major consequences. Once the father was able to ask himself, "Did I make a reasonable decision under the circumstances?" and answer with "Yes," he was able to resolve his guilt issue.

Resolution of one of his worldview threats, his belief in a just and loving God, was one of his initial efforts at making sense of the trauma. At first he rejected God entirely, but later he modified his beliefs and thought of God as a laissez-faire entity who allows evil to flourish and who seldom intervenes in worldly or personal events. His beliefs in a just world also had to undergo some changes in order to assimilate the death of his son: "The world is a reasonably just, predictable, and orderly place that tends to reward hard work, ethics, morality, and altruistic behavior, but not always. On occasion, these values will even be punished. Sometimes shit happens through no fault of your own, and it shows no favorites. Almost everyone will have a bucket or two of shit dumped on them during the course of their lifetime. If you're lucky, the buckets will come during your adult years and they will be spaced out a bit in time so that you will have a chance to recover from one dousing before the next one hits. Between buckets, there are many, many pleasures and blessings in life that can and should be enjoyed. Also, once you have had a bucket dumped on you, you are not exempt from more, nor are you privileged in any way. There is no quota of buckets. Unfortunately, you have as much a chance of having another major bucket dumped on you as does the man standing next to you who has only had a few minor sprinklings. It may not be fair and we may not like it, but until such time as one of us gets elevated to the status of God and changes it, we'll just have to learn to live with it."

Resolution of another one of his worldview threats, his belief that authority figures can be trusted, came when he reframed the event into a damned-if-you-do-and-damned-if-you-don't situation for the physician as well as for himself. "People in authority are frequently presented with damned-if-you-do-and-damned-if-you-don't types of situations and frequently have to make bad decisions. Of course, some authority figures do make mistakes and some are incompetent. But you have to analyze the situation as well as the outcome. If it is a damned-if-you-do-and-damned-if-you-don't type of situation, you need to ask yourself, did he or she make a reasonable (as opposed to 'right') decision under the circumstances? In the case of my son, I certainly understand the bind the physician was in, as I was in the same bind. His decision to not honor my request to kill my son was a reasonable one under the circumstances. Certainly it was not the one I would have preferred, but it was reasonable under the circumstances."

Resolution of the impulse threat posed by his rage came by accepting it as a normal reaction. "I was filled with hate and rage, and I had very strong wishes to retaliate against someone or something. But who? I knew this was wrong, and I felt that as long as I took appropriate precautions, it was unlikely that I would actually lose control and act on those intense wishes. I stayed out of redneck bars and other situations where I thought there was a good chance of somebody hassling me. I also took great care to avoid alcohol. I knew alcohol and the rage I was feeling could be a lethal mix. What really bothered me about my rage was not the rage itself, it was the fact that I could actually enjoy beating someone to death with my bare hands. I recognized this beast within me as dangerous but controllable, and certainly not me. I realized that the beast would eventually be locked back up in its cage, and the intense, sadistic, aggressive wishes would go away. I also realized that the beast had some value. This beast could very well serve a useful purpose if my loved ones' lives or my own life were again threatened. The aggression it unleashes could keep them and me alive in certain situations. I realized that God or evolution, as a way of preserving our species, probably built the beast into us eons ago. I saw it as essentially a normal human reaction that will occur under certain—usually tragic—circumstances. However, knowing and believing all this, I was still quite unnerved by the fact that I could actually enjoy beating someone to death. I am also quite thankful that life didn't present me with any unmanageable situations when I had the beast with me. Now that the beast is back in its cage, it comforts me to know that it is part of me but is not my essence. It can and will be uncaged for survival purposes if my life or my loved ones' lives are ever endangered in the future."

Example Treatment Plan

Name: _____

Date: _____

Each of the following four goals will be accomplished within four months by way of fifteen sessions of therapy with the counselor whose name appears below.

Goal 1: I will reduce the frequency of unwanted intrusive thoughts about my combat experiences from five a day to two or fewer a month.

Goal 2: I will reduce the amount and duration of the distress I experience when I do have an intrusive thought about my combat experiences from six SUDs and four hours of upset (on average) to four SUDs and five minutes of upset (on average).

Goal 3: I will reduce the distress I experience in crowds from eight SUDs (on average) to four SUDs.

Goal 4: I will reduce the generalized level of distress I experience almost every day in almost all situations from five SUDs (on average) to four SUDs.

Participant's Signature _____

Counselor's Signature _____

Phase II

Emotion-Focused Coping-Skills Training

Sessions 3 and 4

Goals:

- Complete a self-assessment to get an idea of how you are doing overall.

- Set the agenda by reviewing your treatment goals.

- Master two emotion-focused coping skills.

- Review the SUD scale.

- Practice the eye-movement technique.

- Practice the relaxation response.

- Negotiate homework assignments. Probable homework for this phase:

    1. Practice inducing the relaxation response at least five times this week as a form of meditation.

    2. Experiment with the relaxation response this week. Try it out at least three times to see if you can use it as an emotion-focused coping device when you find yourself in the five to six SUDs range. Try it as preparation for encountering a known stressor at least twice this week.

3. Experiment with the eye-movement technique this week. Try it out at least five times to see if you can use it as an emotion-focused coping device when you find yourself in the five to six SUDs range.

4. Experiment with combining the eye-movement technique, the relaxation response, and reassuring self-talk as emotion-focused coping devices at least five times this week when you first notice your distress is in the five to six SUDs range.

The first objective of this phase is to review the subjective units of distress (SUD) scale, which will be used to communicate how much distress you are experiencing. (The SUD scale is found on page 7.) The second objective is to learn to use two emotion-focused coping skills to control your distress: the eye-movement technique and the relaxation response. You can assist in this process by completing all agreed-upon homework assignments.

The Eye-Movement Technique and Other Not-Thinking Techniques

What Are Not-thinking Techniques?

Not-thinking techniques are a group of psychological strategies we all use from time to time to stop ourselves from thinking about unpleasant distress-inducing events. These techniques are more commonly referred to as distraction, suppression, or repression.

Aren't Not-Thinking Techniques Bad for Me?

Yes and no. As the old saying goes, there is virtue in moderation. Not-thinking strategies can be overused and cause excessive distress when problems are not addressed that can and should be solved. However, with anxiety disorders the individual usually is not employing not-thinking strategies properly, or not employing them frequently enough.

When Should I Use Not-Thinking Strategies?

Not-thinking strategies should be used to stop or decrease unproductive problem-solving, or what is more commonly known as worry. By definition, worry involves thinking about a distressful situation in an attempt to solve a problem, or an anticipated problem, and exaggerating the potential negative consequences (catastrophizing) of the problem. Worry also frequently involves dwelling on a problem and searching for solutions when the solutions that do exist are outside the individual's control.

How Do I Decide if I Should Use a Not-Thinking Technique?

To decide whether or not to continue thinking about a problem or turn to a not-thinking strategy, ask yourself the following questions:

- What's the most likely outcome if this problem continues?

- What's the worst possible outcome, how likely is this to occur, and can I manage it if it does occur?

- Are the solutions to the problem under my control, or are they outside of my control for now?

If you answer in any of the following ways, you should probably choose a not-thinking strategy to stop the worry:

- The most likely outcome is a good one, so there is no value in focusing on unlikely negative outcomes.

- The most likely outcome is a negative one, but even at the worst, it's only an inconvenience—a hassle—that I can certainly live with.

- There are no solutions to the problem. (Or:) What solutions exist are outside of my control for the present.

What Not-Thinking Technique Should I Use?

Most people suppress worry by engaging in a pleasant activity that captures their attention such as competitive sports, reading a good book, pursuing an engrossing hobby, visiting friends, or working. Another way to reduce worry is to compartmentalize it. Set aside a specific time and place each day to worry intensely about your problems—but stubbornly refuse to worry at other times or in other places. Thought-stopping and the eye-movement technique (below) are two other not-thinking techniques that you may find helpful.

What Is Thought-Stopping?

Thought-stopping is a technique some individuals find useful for controlling worry. In thought-stopping, your worry is first suppressed when your therapist yells "Stop" while you are worrying. Next, you yell "Stop," first aloud and then silently when you worry, demonstrating to yourself that you can interfere with worrisome thoughts without the assistance of your therapist. You may also be encouraged to snap a rubber band you wear around your wrist at the same time you silently yell "Stop." This induces mild pain and facilitates the refocusing of your attention away from the worrisome thoughts. Next, you will be encouraged to further suppress the worry with pleasant thoughts and activities.

What Is the Eye-Movement Technique?

The eye-movement technique is a relatively new anxiety-management technique that was discovered by Dr. Francine Shapiro. Dr. Shapiro added other processes to the original technique, theorized about why it worked, and then promoted the entire package under the name "eye-movement desensitization and reprocessing" (EMDR). The eye-movement technique is deceptively simple; all it requires is moving your eyes rapidly from side to side about twenty-five times while imagining, thinking, or worrying about stressful life events. Often this quickly leads to marked reductions in the amount of distress produced by the worrisome thoughts and images.

Clinical experience indicates that for some individuals the eye movements change the visual component of a worry or a distressing memory. For example, the worrisome images fade away, become blurred, appear more distant, or appear less real after the person has engaged in a series of rapid eye movements. Most individuals, however, report the eye movements simply block their distress-inducing images and thoughts: "I can't imagine the problem or worry about it when I move my eyes back and forth like that."

The eye-movement technique does not work for everyone. About 75 percent of those who try it derive some benefit from it. The fact that the gains are often substantial and occur so rapidly makes the eye-movement technique worth trying in most cases, however.

Is the Eye-Movement Technique Better than the Relaxation Response or Rational Thinking?

Yes and no. For many people, the eye-movement technique appears better at reducing distress when it is in the high to severe range (seven to ten SUDs). The relaxation response and rational thinking appear superior to the eye-movement technique when the distress is in the mild to moderate range (four to six SUDs). The relaxation response appears superior to the eye-movement technique and rational thinking in achieving the deepest levels of comfort and relaxation (one to three SUDs).

The eye-movement technique, the relaxation response, and rational thinking can be used together. In most cases, the three different approaches complement one another and the individual benefits from combining all three to cope with his or her excessive emotional distress. Since it is impossible to tell beforehand which of these techniques will work for an individual, it is best to try out all three.

Can I Use the Eye-Movement Technique on My Own?

Yes. The eye-movement technique, the relaxation response, and rational thinking should all be placed under your control and used outside the treatment sessions to manage your distress.

Tips for Relaxation Training

At one time early in our lives, we all probably knew how to relax, but gradually, many of us lose this ability as we grow older, become more and more achievement-oriented, and begin to abuse stimulants such as caffeine and nicotine. Our innate ability to calm ourselves down, rest, and relax becomes increasingly difficult in a highly competitive world that encourages and rewards achievement and aggression. Certainly hard work, striving to get ahead, and industriousness are all laudable traits, but sometimes they can be overdone. Our work ethic can and does go awry from time to time, which can lead to chronic and excessive stress and possible somatic symptoms such as headaches and ulcers. As the old saying goes, there can be too much of a good thing.

Cognitive-behavioral therapy incorporates what is called relaxation training in an effort to help people restore a healthy balance between their achievement strivings and their need to relax, rest, and replenish themselves. More specifically, relaxation training is designed to teach people how to induce the relaxation or quieting response so that they can keep themselves reasonably calm in competitive (for example, test-taking) situations. The relaxation response can be learned in ways other than through relaxation training: yoga, transcendental meditation, autogenic training, hypnosis, biofeedback therapy, and some forms of physical exercise. The main advantages of relaxation training are: it is simpler to learn and takes less time than some of the other approaches, it is not couched in Eastern mysticism, and it can be applied in virtually any situation that a person might encounter.

Main points to keep in mind as you induce the relaxation response:

- There is no right way or wrong way to induce the relaxation response.
  You will be introduced to a variety of procedures designed to induce the relaxation response, including progressive muscle relaxation, passive muscle relaxation, breathing exercises, and directed visual imagery. Your task is to try them all, experiment a bit, and come up with the procedure(s) that works the best for you.

- The relaxation response is a learned skill and like any learned skill it requires practice.
  With practice, you will find that the relaxation response becomes easier and quicker to induce, and you will become more adept at inducing it in more and more difficult situations. With sufficient practice, you should be able to induce the relaxation response in a matter of a minute or two. Sometimes it can be induced in a matter of seconds.

- Make it easy on yourself.
  When you first start out learning to induce the relaxation response, you should be reasonably comfortable when you begin; don't attempt to induce it if you are highly distressed until you have developed sufficient skill to handle high levels of stress.

- Understand that it does not always work.
  Like any learned skill, sometimes you will be "on" and you will be able to quickly and easily induce the relaxation response. Other times you will be

"off" and will not be able to relax yourself very quickly, easily, or deeply. Practice does improve one's ability to induce the relaxation response, but there will still be times when the response will not come as easily as you would like.

- Make it fun.
  Although you do need to practice, don't overdo it. In most cases, you will need to induce the relaxation response a minimum of five times a week. There is no maximum, but stop when you feel that it is getting boring or bothersome.

- Intrusive thoughts should be expected.
  You are likely to have bothersome, distracting thoughts come to mind that will momentarily capture your attention and increase your stress while you are inducing the relaxation response. That's to be expected. Probably the best way to handle them is to simply allow them to pass in and then pass out of your mind without devoting much attention to them or damning yourself for having them. With practice, intrusive thoughts are less likely to occur and will become less intrusive.

- Your relaxation response does not have to be perfect to be beneficial.
  Although some people are able to achieve profound levels of mental and physical relaxation, not everyone will be able to do so, and you don't have to reach extremely deep levels of relaxation to experience the benefits. Becoming adept at inducing mild to moderate degrees of relaxation is usually sufficient to accomplish what most people want to accomplish in cognitive- behavioral therapy.

- Breathing properly is very important in inducing the relaxation response. People often take many rapid, shallow breaths when frightened—this is called hyperventilation. Hyperventilation, however, actually can create anxious feelings in your body by putting too much oxygen in your blood. Probably the best way to prevent hyperventilation is to take a normal breath and then force yourself to exhale slowly by saying "R-e-e-e-l-a-a-x-x-x" slowly and gently to yourself two or three times before taking the next breath. This will slow down your breathing and prevent the hyperventilation-induced feelings of anxiety from occurring.

- If you have chronic and excessive high levels of stress, you need to practice the relaxation response at least once a day (preferably twice) on a regular basis.
  If you are innately high-strung, you will have to integrate the relaxation response into your daily life. Otherwise the gains you make from relaxation training are likely to be short-lived.

So I'm Relaxed, Now What?

There are a number of different ways that you can put the relaxation response to use once you have mastered it. Four of the most common ways are as follows:

1. It can be used as a form of meditation.

   Many people find that practicing the relaxation response once or twice a day on a regular basis can be very helpful in reducing the incidence of chronic stress-related symptoms such as headaches, gastritis, and so on. Ten or fifteen minutes once or twice a day is usually all the time that is needed, but it must be induced on a regular basis for the benefits to be maintained.

2. It can be used to reduce insomnia.

   Inducing the relaxation response in bed as a way of preparing oneself for sleep often proves useful in reducing restlessness and sleeplessness. Again, this requires it to be practiced on a fairly regular basis.

3. It can be used to control stress in certain stressful situations such as test taking, public speaking, or job interviewing.

   The relaxation response can be used to prevent the arousal of excessive stress in many situations if the individual practices prior to entering the stressful situation. For example, arriving at a prospective employer's office twenty minutes early and self-inducing the relaxation response while you wait to meet him or her can be very helpful in keeping down the stress you do experience during the interview.

   It also can be used to reduce the stress you experience while you are actually in the stressful situation. For example, you might take a minute or two to self-induce the relaxation response by means of an abbreviated relaxation exercise while you are in the process of taking an important exam, if you notice that your stress is becoming uncomfortably high.

4. It can be used in conjunction with anxiety-management training to eliminate or greatly reduce simple phobias, social phobias, and chronic performance anxiety.

   Examples include fear of flying, severe test anxiety, and excessive fear of making a social error. Anxiety-management training is a procedure in which the person becomes relaxed, vividly imagines stressful scenes, and then is taught to use the relaxation response and what is called "rational" self-talk to calm himself or herself down. Once the person can control stress in imagined situations, he is gradually introduced to the same situation in real life, where again he is taught to control his or her stress through the use of the relaxation response and rational self-talk.

Phase III

Assimilation Work

Session 5

Goals:

- Complete a self-assessment to get an idea of how you are doing overall.

- Set the agenda by reviewing your treatment goals and your homework.

- Develop and begin applying rational-thinking and assimilation strategies to control your distress when you're exposed to anxiety-provoking cues.

- Develop rational thinking.

- Develop assimilation strategies.

- Review traumatic memories.

- Negotiate homework assignments. Probable homework for this phase:

  1. Continue practicing the relaxation response as a form of meditation on a daily basis.

  2. Use a combination of the eye-movement technique, the relaxation response, and rational thinking as emotion-focused coping devices this week whenever your distress gets into the five to six SUDs range.

  3. Review your traumatic memories by way of the tape recording made of your in-session review. Be sure to use assimilation and rational-thinking strategies to manage your distress throughout your review.

The objective of this phase is to develop rational-thinking and assimilation strategies to help control distress during your exposure work. If assimilation and rational-thinking strategies are insufficient to keep your SUDs at six and a half or below during reviews of your traumatic memories, then terminate this phase and proceed to the brief-exposure work phase (Phase IV).

Cognitive Problem-Solving

Cognitive problem-solving is nothing more than finding solutions for problems you encounter. It is a critical skill we all must master, since problems are an inevitable part of our lives.

Steps in Cognitive Problem-Solving

1. Define the problem.
   In this step, you must answer the questions, "What do I want?" and "What obstacles are in my way?" Errors in this step occur when the first question is confused with, "What *should* I want?" Another error is to infer malicious intent on the part of obstacles when none exist. This leads to demanding that things be different: "He shouldn't be that way." This, in turn, can interfere with finding a way of getting around the obstacle.

2. Identify possible solutions.
   Solutions to problems can be classified as attack strategies, avoidance strategies, or negotiating strategies. Different problems require different strategies. Good solutions can be overlooked if solutions are habitually drawn from only one or two of these categories.

3. Select and implement one of the solutions.
   In this step, you must evaluate the short-term and long-term consequences of your potential solutions, and then implement the best of several imperfect solutions. Sometimes errors are made when solutions are implemented that solve immediate problems but later worsen other problems. More often, errors occur because too much time is spent mulling over potential solutions looking for a perfect solution. This is particularly true in the anxiety disorders, where excessive thinking and not enough doing is the rule rather than the exception.

4. Evaluate the outcome.
   In this step, evaluate how effective your solution was in solving the problem. If the problem was not solved satisfactorily, select another possible solution and implement it after checking to see that you accurately defined the problem. Then evaluate the effectiveness of the second solution. Repeat this process until the problem is solved. Errors usually occur when, instead of focusing on problem-solving, you focus on blaming others, damning the obstacle, or berating yourself.

Tips for Effective Cognitive Problem-Solving

- Apply the Serenity Prayer: "God, grant me the serenity to accept the things I cannot change, the courage to change the things I can, and the wisdom to know the difference."

- If the problem is changeable, apply the four basic steps identified above.

- If the problem is unchangeable, apply not-thinking techniques and other emotion-focused coping skills such as the relaxation response and rational thinking.

Rational Thinking and the ABC Model

The "A" in the ABC model refers to the activating event, such as being criticized by your boss. The "B" refers to the beliefs and the irrational self-talk that follows: "No one likes me. I am about to be fired. How awful." The "C" refers to the emotional consequences provoked by the self-talk, such as agitated depression. There can also be a "D" in the model, which refers to the disputes that can be used to correct irrational self-talk, such as, "Some people like me, and even my boss likes me at times. Besides, it's not that important that everyone like me; it is highly unlikely that I'll lose my job. Even if I do, it is not a catastrophe—just highly inconvenient."

Note that irrational self-talk is often spoken in a very terse and abbreviated fashion. For example, "Oh, no," might be all that is said to oneself, but this may mean, "Oh, no! Here we go again. I know I'm going to fail and fail miserably. Everything is going to go wrong, and there is nothing I can do about it. How unfair." Also, irrational self-talk is often spoken so frequently and habitually that the person isn't consciously aware he or she is thinking in an irrational fashion. The person's irrational beliefs, from which the self-talk springs, are usually even further from conscious awareness.

Excessive fear and anxiety are usually provoked by irrational self-talk in the form of grave-danger messages such as, "If I keep on this way, I'm certain to lose my job, my girlfriend, and all my friends." Depression is usually provoked by irrational self-talk in the form of helpless, hopeless, worthless, or grave-loss messages such as, "Everything is bad. It's going to get much worse. There's nothing I can do about it, and I am a horribly incompetent person for allowing it to happen." Anger is usually provoked by irrational self-talk in the form of grave-injustice messages such as, "It's terribly unfair and unjust how my husband, my father, and my children treat me. I can't stand it." People seldom experience pure anxiety, anger, or depression, however. They are far more likely to have mixtures of these emotions provoked by combinations of worthless, hopeless, helpless, grave-loss, grave-injustice, and grave-danger messages.

The ABC Model, Part One: Activating Events ("A") and Beliefs and Irrational Self-Talk ("B"), with the Emotional Consequence ("C") of Anxiety or Fear

Examples of "A"	"B": Beliefs	"B": Irrational Self-Talk
Presence of a phobic object such as snakes	My life is in danger.	"I'm going to have a heart attack."
Presence of a significant other such as a potential employer or a potential friend	I must be loved, liked, respected by everyone all the time.	"I'm going to fail and that would be awful and humiliating."
Presence of psychological distress such as anxiety or depression	I must be perfect.	"I'm going to go crazy."

The ABC Model, Part Two: Activating Events ("A") and Beliefs and Irrational Self-Talk ("B"), with the Emotional Consequence ("C") of Depression

Examples of "A"	"B": Beliefs	"B": Irrational Self-Talk
Loss or anticipated loss of a job	I must be perfect.	"How awful that I lost my job. There's nothing I can do about it. It's never going to get any better. I must be an incompetent fool."
Loss or anticipated loss of a relationship	I must be loved, liked, respected by everyone all the time.	"I'm not as smart or as attractive as I want to be. How awful. There's nothing I can do about it and it's only going to get worse. I must be a horrible social misfit."
Loss or anticipated loss of social status	I must be perfect; I must be respected.	"I'm never going to amount to anything. I'll never recover, and there's nothing I can do about it."

The ABC Model, Part Three: Activating Events ("A") and Beliefs and Irrational Self-Talk ("B"), with the Emotional Consequence ("C") of Anger

Examples of "A"	"B": Beliefs	"B": Irrational Self-Talk
Obstacles placed in a person's path that hinder him from achieving the goals he is striving to reach	The world should be perfectly fair and just.	"It's horribly unfair that I didn't receive the promotion I deserved."
Loss or anticipated loss of a job, relationship, or social status	The world should be exactly as I wish it to be.	"It's terribly unjust that I get discriminated against because I'm not as attractive or intelligent as others are."
Discrepancy between ideal self and real self	I should get what I want when I want it.	"He's in my way and is gravely endangering me and my principles. I must attack."

The ABC Model, Part Four: Activating Events ("A") and Beliefs and Irrational Self-Talk ("B"), with the Emotional Consequence ("C") of Guilt and Shame

Examples of "A"	"B": Beliefs	"B": Irrational Self-Talk
Discrepancy between ideal self and real self	I must be perfect.	"I'm completely worthless and no one could possibly like or respect me for what I've done or failed to do."
Criticism by a coworker or friend	I must be loved, liked, respected by everyone all the time.	"They don't like me. I've done something wrong. I'm worthless."
Failing to keep a promise	People, God, do not forgive crimes or sins of this nature.	"I'm unacceptable. No one could think well of me, ever. Even God has forsaken me."

Five Common Irrational Beliefs

Listed below are five of the most common beliefs (B) that result in irrational self-talk and excessive emotional distress. The words turning these beliefs into irrational self-talk are underlined. As you read these beliefs, develop arguments against them that correct their irrational nature.

1. I must be perfect and never make any social, vocational, or academic mistakes. If I do, I am a horribly incompetent and worthless person, and terrible things will most certainly befall me.

2. I must be loved, liked, and respected by certain people all the time. If not, I am horrible, and terrible things will most certainly happen to me. It is terribly unfair and unjust that they don't love, like, and respect me as they should.

3. The world should be perfectly just and fair. If it isn't, it is a horrible and unjust tragedy, and those people responsible for the injustice should be vilified and severely punished.

4. I should get what I want when I want it, and the world should be just exactly as I believe it should be. If not, it is a horrible and unjust tragedy, and those people responsible for the injustice should be found out and severely punished.

5. Because my life or the life of someone else was endangered once, I should always regard the world as an extremely dangerous place and never trust anyone ever again.

Note: A person is seldom consciously aware of his or her beliefs. These beliefs are assumptions people make about themselves and about the world in which they live. Usually, these beliefs have never been translated into words, but they can be readily inferred by examining the individual's irrational self-talk.

Five Common Distortions in Thinking

Listed below are five common distortions in thinking. The words that distort the self-talk are underlined. As you read the examples, correct the irrational nature of the self-talk, making it more rational or realistic.

1. Overgeneralizing. In this type of thinking, the person usually makes dire predictions for the future based on a single negative event such as, "I got turned down for that job; I'll never get a job." The person can also globally condemn himself or herself based on a single negative comparison such as, "I lost the job, therefore I must be a loser," or "I'm not as pretty as Betty; I'm ugly," or "I'm not as smart as Joe; I'm stupid." This same type of thinking can occur with respect to judgments made about other people such as, "He made a mistake; he's a loser."

2. Awfulizing. This type of thinking often accompanies overgeneralizing and involves exaggerating the significance of a negative event. "Jim doesn't love me anymore. No one will ever love me again. I'm certain I'll be alone the rest of my life, which is just horrible."

3. Overpersonalizing. This type of thinking involves a great deal of mind reading and an exaggerated sense of importance. For example, concluding "The boss doesn't like me," because the boss didn't smile at you when he or she was preoccupied with personal problems at the time. Another example is the conclusion, "Everyone is gossiping about me at work," when actually you may be of little concern to your coworkers. Elements of overgeneralizing and awfulizing are almost always present when overpersonalizing occurs.

4. Discrediting and discounting. This type of thinking involves rejecting positive experiences because they don't count for one reason or another. For example, a person might hold on to the belief they are incompetent by discrediting his or her performance ratings with thoughts such as, "I was just lucky," or "If they really knew me, they wouldn't think much of me."

5. "Shoulding" and "musting." This type of thinking involves demanding that the world (or yourself) should, ought, or must be exactly as you want it to be. For example, "My boss should recognize me for my hard work, and it is terribly unjust that he doesn't."

Correcting Irrational Self-Talk

Instructions: The following is an example of how excessive stress in a job interview can be generated by irrational self-talk and mental imagery. This example also illustrates the relationship between self-talk and the underlying beliefs from which the self-talk springs. As you read, practice generating disputes to each piece of irrational self-talk, labeled "(a)," "(b)," and so on. Possible answers are listed at the end.

A	Activating Event	Approaching the office for a job interview.
B	automatic, abbreviated self-talk and images	"Uh, oh. Here we go again," accompanied by a mental image of a skid-row alcoholic.
	the self-talk and images decoded	(a) "I absolutely must do well in this interview. (b) I must appear calm, cool, and collected. (c) Any sign of anxiety will most certainly (d) cause me to fail the interview. (e) I cannot afford to fail or make any mistakes. (f) If I do, I will certainly end up a skid-row alcoholic."
	Beliefs underlying the self-talk	I must be perfect. I cannot afford to make any mistakes. The world is an extremely dangerous, intolerant, unforgiving place.

C	Emotional Consequences	intense anxiety (a SUD rating of eight).
D	Disputes	(a) "That's unproductive thinking. Although I certainly would prefer to do well in the job interview, it is not mandatory. I'm human, not a social robot. Like everybody else, I inevitably make some social errors of one type or another in most social settings."
		(b, c, d) "That's unproductive thinking. Although it might be preferable to be completely calm, it is not mandatory. Most people are nervous in job interviews. Being nervous is expected, and some anxiety is good. It keeps me sharp. Besides, being extremely calm could be interpreted as disinterest, not taking the interview seriously, and so on. The anxiety I experience may well be uncomfortable, but it will be short-lived and it is not dangerous."
		(e, f) "That's unproductive thinking. I certainly would prefer to do well in the interview, but I can afford to fail because failure is an inevitable part of life; everyone fails. The trick is to master the art of failure. Babe Ruth hit the most home runs but he also led the league in strikeouts. In order for him to hit those home runs he had to learn to not be bothered by strikeouts. There will be other opportunities to get a hit even if I strike out this time at bat."

Here's another example of how to correct irrational self-talk. This time, the example shows how traumatic war memories can contribute to excessive distress in everyday life. Again, as you read, practice generating disputes to each piece of irrational self-talk, labeled "(a)," "(b)," and so on. Possible answers are listed at the end.

A	Activating Event	Approaching the office for a job interview.
B	automatic, abbreviated self-talk and images	"Uh, oh. Here we go again," accompanied by a mental image of a friend bleeding to death from a wound suffered in Vietnam.
	the self-talk and images decoded	"This interviewer is probably (a) just like my old CO, in fact, I'm sure of it. (b) He doesn't care about people at all. He only cares about his job. (c) That's the way all bosses are, and (d) that's terribly unfair. (e) That's exactly why Bill died—because the CO sent us out on a needless mission to make himself look good. (f) Bosses are dangerous, very dangerous; they will get you killed. My God, my anger and my anxiety are getting out of control. (g) I'm in grave danger of dying. (h) I'm certain to fail the interview. I'm done for again (i) and (j) I can't afford to fail."
	Beliefs underlying the self-talk	The world should be perfectly fair and just. People can't be trusted. The world is a very dangerous place. I must be perfect

C	Emotional Consequences	intense anxiety mixed with anger (a SUD rating of eight).
D	Disputes	(a, b, c) "That's overgeneralizing. It's possible this guy is like my CO in overemphasizing his job at the expense of concern for people, but it's just as likely that he is a decent or good manager who tries to find a healthy balance between the two. It's best to give him the benefit of the doubt. I'll just have to wait and see what kind of man and boss he is. Certainly a few bosses are that way, but not all."
		(d) "That's awfulizing. It would certainly be unfortunate if this guy turns out to be too job-focused for my liking, but it's not a terrible injustice if he does. Again, I'll just have to wait and see."
		(e, f) "That's overgeneralizing. A poor CO in war can be a contributing cause of casualties, but this is civilian life. The chance of this guy doing something stupid or self-serving that could get me killed is highly unlikely."
		(g) "That's awfulizing. My anger and my anxiety are certainly uncomfortable, but they are not endangering my life."
		(h, i, j) "That's overgeneralizing. Just because I've done poorly in some interviews doesn't mean I will foul up this one. After all, I have done well in some. Perhaps this will be one of those times. And even if I don't do well, it will not be the end of the world, just an inconvenience. I can generate other job leads if this one doesn't pan out.

The "Catastrophe Scale" Exercise

Depicted below is a "catastrophe and social injustice scale" about which most people in American culture could agree. Most people would regard the loss of millions of lives to be a greater catastrophe than being wrongfully imprisoned, which in turn would be regarded as more of a catastrophe than being passed over for a promotion, and so on. In peacetime, most of the stressors we encounter are in the zero to ten-point range—minor irritants and hassles. Yet we all sometimes evaluate these common ten-pointers as major catastrophes and consequently experience excessive distress. As you read the scale, evaluate your current stressors. Are they major catastrophes? Are you threatened with loss of life or loss of freedom, or are the stressors at the lower end of the continuum? Give your stressors a rational catastrophe/injustice rating. Then, establish your *own* catastrophe scale by listing events that have actually happened to you. When you encounter your stressors in day-to-day activities, use your scale to ask yourself, "How bad is it, really?" or "Compared to my fifty-point catastrophe, how bad is it?" You are likely to find yourself reducing your distress by more rationally evaluating your everyday stressors.

Injustice Rating	Example Stressor	Personal Stressor
100	A nuclear war breaks out and millions of people lose their lives.	
75	Your child dies a prolonged and agonizing death at the age of five.	
50	You are imprisoned for five years for a crime you did not commit based on false testimony of others.	
30	You are libeled by friends or family and it results in the loss of your job.	
20	You are passed over for a promotion because of racial bias.	
5	You are treated rudely by a store clerk.	
0	It's raining and you wanted sunshine.	

My Personal Worksheet for Correcting Irrational Self-Talk

The following form can be used to identify irrational self-talk and irrational images you may be using in your everyday life. Pick a specific day(s), time(s), and situation(s) you are likely to experience excess distress and closely monitor what you actually say to yourself under these circumstances. Begin the process by noting the amount and type of excessive distress you are experiencing (referred to earlier as "C," or emotional consequence), then note the event(s) that was occurring just prior to the excessive stress reaction (referred to earlier as "A," or activating event), and then note the irrational self-talk. Try to infer what the self-talk means and what the underlying beliefs (referred to earlier as "B") are. Dispute or argue against any irrational self-talk you find.

Emotional consequences; SUDs level: _____

Activating event, such as thinking about or attempting to speak in front of a small group of strangers:

_____

Irrational self-talk, such as, "Oh, no," which to you might mean, "Oh, no, I'm going to become tongue-tied again, or do something even worse. I just know it. I'm going to make a complete and utter fool of myself. The embarrassment will be unbearable. I won't be able to handle it. Everyone will think I'm stupid, and that would be horrible."

_____

_____

_____

Disputes, such as, "I might make a mistake and stutter some, but it's not a certainty. Besides, even if I do make a social error of some type, it's not likely to be a big one. It's far more likely to be one of those garden-variety types of social errors we all make on a regular basis. And even if I do something like stumble over my words, it's not going to kill me. It's only going to cause me a little bit of discomfort and embarrassment that will last for only a short while. I can handle it."

_____

_____

_____

Phase IV

Brief Exposure and Assimilation Work

Sessions 6 to 11

Goals:

- Complete a self-assessment to get an idea of how you are doing overall.

- Set the agenda by reviewing your treatment goals and your homework.

- Reduce your emotional reactivity to distress-inducing cues by way of brief-exposure work.

- Plan and conduct a brief-exposure exercise.

- Negotiate homework assignments. Probable homework for this phase:

    1. Continue to practice inducing the relaxation response on a daily basis as a form of meditation.

    2. Continue to use a combination of the eye-movement technique, the relaxation response, and rational thinking as emotion-focused coping skills whenever your distress gets into the five-to-six SUDs range, particularly when these emotional reactions are triggered by encounters with cues related to your anxiety disorder.

    3. Conduct at least three, and preferably five or more, imaginal brief-exposure exercises using the tape made in your therapy session. You can also do it on your own, without the aid of the tape, if you prefer.

4. Conduct three, preferably five or more, in vivo brief-exposure exercises this week, with at least five exposure trials per exercise. In other words, approach a situation related to your anxiety disorder in real life. Expose yourself to these anxiety-disorder-related environmental cues, conjure up the visual images and irrational thoughts related to your anxiety disorder, and purposely push yourself to between five and six SUDs, but no more than that. Then apply the three emotion-focused coping skills you have mastered to reduce the distress to about four SUDs or so. Repeat this calm-stress-calm sequence five to ten times, more if you have the time.

Note: Be sure to apply the CAP principle (explained below) throughout these exercises. Expect to see a coping effect and a desensitization effect develop toward the end of the week.

The objective of this phase is to reduce your excessive distress by briefly exposing yourself to cues that provoke the distress, such as memories, worries, sensations, objects, or situations. Brief-exposure exercises should be conducted initially in your imagination and in your therapist's presence. Later, taped recordings of these exercises should be used to conduct brief-exposure exercises on your own. Still later, brief-exposure exercises should be conducted in real life. Once strong coping effects have developed, you should begin prolonged-exposure work. A coping effect is defined as an increase in the ease, quickness, and confidence with which you calm yourself down once you're stressed by anxiety-disorder-related cues.

Sometimes individuals can omit the brief-exposure work phase and move directly into the prolonged-exposure work phase. This will shorten the duration of treatment, but doing so can also overwhelm some people, causing some undesirable side effects such as an intensification of their depression. Brief-exposure work should only be omitted if you can keep your distress at six and a half SUDs or below by way of rational-thinking strategies when you're exposed to anxiety-disorder-related cues.

A Guide to Brief-Exposure Work

What Occurs in Brief-Exposure Work?

You will be trained in several emotion-focused coping skills to help you manage your distress during exposure work. First, you will be taught to induce the relaxation response. Then, stressful situations as well as the irrational self-talk that induces the stress will be identified. Next, you will vividly imagine the stressful situations, talk to yourself in an irrational fashion, and purposely generate moderate amounts of distress. The relaxation response, the eye-movement technique, and rational thinking will be used to reduce this distress, with this relax-stress-relax sequence repeated four or five times per exposure exercise. A brief-exposure exercise will be conducted every therapy session during this phase of treatment, with approximately five exercises conducted every week as homework. Initially, these exercises will be conducted in your imagination. Later they will be conducted in real-life situations. With sufficient repetition, you will become quite adept at calming yourself down under more and more trying circumstances, demonstrating what is called a coping effect. Prolonged-exposure work commences once a strong coping effect is noted.

Basic Steps in Brief-Exposure work

- You should begin your brief-exposure work by imagining stress-inducing situations, sensations, thoughts, or memories that are capable of eliciting moderate amounts of distress (five to six SUDs).

- Strive to produce five to six SUDs in each brief-exposure trial. Employ the emotion-focused coping skills to calm yourself back down to about four SUDs before moving on to the next exposure trial. The duration of each exposure trial should be brief—five minutes or less. Usually, five exposure trials constitute a brief-exposure exercise. Tape recordings made of the in-session exposure work should be used to structure subsequent exposure exercises assigned as homework.

- Increase the duration of the brief-exposure trials and include more and more distress-inducing cues as coping and desensitization effects become evident.

- Move from imaginal brief-exposure work to in vivo (in real life) brief-exposure work as coping and desensitization effects become evident.

- The transition from imaginal brief-exposure to prolonged-exposure in real life should be guided by the CAP principle: The "C" stands for, "challenge, but never overwhelm." In other words, push yourself to between five and six SUDs, but no more than that. You should proceed to the next step in the exposure sequence when you can no longer readily provoke five to six SUDs at the current step in the sequence. The "A" stands for, "apply the emotion-focused coping skills to reduce your distress, never resort to escape to do so." The "P" stands for, "practice, practice, practice." In other words, continue conducting exposure exercises until strong coping and desensitization effects develop.

Hierarchies

Hierarchies of stressful events can help keep your distress in the moderate (5 to 6 SUDs) range when you conduct brief-exposure work. In hierarchy construction, you take an event that is quite stressful for you, such as test-taking or public speaking, and break the stressful situation down into a series of stressful scenes or situations that go from mildly distressing to extremely distressing. The number of scenes constructed can be as few as two or as many as one hundred, but four or five scenes are usually sufficient. Usually it is best to begin your exposure work with a scene in the middle of the hierarchy. If the selected scene proves insufficient to provoke the desired 5 to 6 SUDs during your exposure work, then select another scene higher up in the hierarchy. If it provokes more than 6 SUDs, then select a scene lower in the hierarchy. Below is an example of a five-scene hierarchy dealing with test-taking anxiety.

Stress Scene #1

I am sitting in my apartment studying, and I begin thinking about an exam that is a couple of days away. I think such thoughts as, "I'll really mess up again. I know it. I just know it. My anxiety is going to get out of control, and my mind will go blank. Damn."

Stress Scene #2

I'm in my apartment the morning of the exam, getting ready to go to school. I begin to think about the exam and say to myself, "I know I'm going to screw up, I just know it. God, how awful. Everybody will think I am brain damaged or something, and there goes grad school right out the window. Look how anxious I am already! What am I going to do?"

Stress Scene #3

I arrive at the classroom just before the test. Other people are milling around, some cramming, some quizzing each other, and some are just sitting around. I overhear a question someone asks, and realize I don't know the answer. I begin thinking, "I'm really uptight now. Look how my hands are sweating. I wonder if anyone will notice. I don't know the answer to that question. I probably studied all the wrong things again! I know I'm going to mess up! So much for grad school! God, I can't stand it."

Stress Scene #4

I am taking the exam, and I notice the length of the test and say to myself, "I've got to hurry, because I probably won't get through with it if I don't." I can't think of the answer to a question, and I know that I know the answer, and I say to myself, "God, I'm really messing up. There goes my mind. I can't think anymore! My anxiety is out of hand! I wonder if I'm going to faint and make a fool of myself!" I run across another question I don't know the answer to, and I say to myself, "I'm really messing up now. Everybody thinks I'm a dunce! So much for grad school. Might as well pack it in right now! What's wrong with me?"

Stress Scene #5

"Time is running out for the exam and for me," I say to myself. Several other students are finishing up, the clock on the wall says it's getting late. The instructor says, "Time is about up." And I say to myself, "I had better hurry! What's the use. I'm really messing up! My anxiety is out of sight. I can't think! There goes grad school. My instructor thinks I'm retarded! I've wasted my time, the instructor's time, and my parents' money! Damn, I can't wait to get out of here."

Prolonged Exposure and Assimilation Work

Sessions 12 and 13

Goals:

- Complete a self-assessment to get an idea of how you are doing overall.

- Set the agenda by reviewing your treatment goals and your homework.

- Further reduce your emotional reactivity to cues related to your anxiety disorder by way of prolonged-exposure exercises.

- Plan and conduct prolonged-exposure work.

- Negotiate homework assignments. Probable homework for this phase:

    1. Continue to practice inducing the relaxation response on a daily basis as a form of meditation. Also, use the relaxation response to prepare yourself for a known stressor at least twice this week.

    2. Continue to use the combination of the eye-movement technique, the relaxation response, and rational thinking to cope with excessive stress reactions provoked by encounters with anxiety-disorder related cues.

    3. Conduct at least three imaginal prolonged-exposure exercises this week, and use the tape we made in here today to structure the exercises. Be sure to follow the principles of prolonged exposure: Push yourself to about six SUDs and keep yourself there for as long as possible. You can and should use

rational thinking to manage your distress, but hold off on using the eye-movement technique and the relaxation response until the desensitization effect becomes evident. Wait until you find you can't keep your distress at the six SUDs level anymore, and it has fallen to about four or four and a half. Then you can polish off your distress using the eye-movement technique and the relaxation response, then terminate the exercise. Be sure to wait until the desensitization effect has occurred, however. With sufficient brief-exposure work, you should find the desensitization effect setting in after twenty minutes, or maybe thirty minutes, of prolonged-exposure work. You should notice the desensitization effect setting in much earlier toward the end of the week, maybe after five or ten minutes of prolonged-exposure work.

4. Conduct at least three in vivo (in real life) prolonged-exposure exercises this week: put yourself in anxiety-disorder-related situations and then review the visual images, the thoughts, and the sensations all at the same time. Try to push yourself to six SUDs and keep yourself there for as long as possible. You can manage your distress during the prolonged-exposure exercise by rational thinking, but hold off on the use of the eye-movement technique and relaxation response until a desensitization effect becomes evident. Wait until your SUD drops to four or four and a half, despite all your efforts to keep the numbers up, and then polish off your distress using the eye-movement technique and the relaxation response, then terminate the exposure exercise. The desensitization effect should set in after about thirty minutes, maybe sooner, given the amount of imaginal prolonged-exposure work you have done.

The objective of this phase is to further reduce your emotional reactivity to anxiety-disorder related cues by way of prolonged-exposure work. Your reactivity should have been substantially reduced by the brief-exposure work you conducted in the previous phase. Prolonged-exposure exercises should be conducted initially in the presence of your therapist and in your imagination. Later, tape recordings made of these exercises will be used for you to conduct prolonged-exposure work on your own. Still later, you will conduct the exercises in real life. Strong desensitization effects should develop from these exercises, meaning that your anxiety-disorder-related cues should provoke significantly less distress than they did before you began the exposure exercise.

What Is Prolonged-Exposure Work?

Prolonged exposure is a therapeutic strategy where you remain for a lengthy period of time in a situation that provokes excessive amounts of distress. For example, if you were suffering from claustrophobia (an excessive fear of small and confined places), you might stay in an elevator for an hour or two as a means of reducing your fear.

What Is Meant by "Titrated" Prolonged Exposure?

This is simply prolonged-exposure work that you conduct after you've undergone a sufficient amount of brief-exposure work to have produced strong coping effects. The initial titrated prolonged-exposure exercise is likely to last about a half hour. The duration of the exercises usually drops to ten minutes or less after you conduct two or three of them. Titrated prolonged-exposure work is usually conducted in the therapist's office and in your imagination before you conduct it in the real world. For instance, if you suffered from an irrational fear of bridges, you might (while in the therapist's office) vividly imagine yourself driving across a bridge until your anxiety dropped to about four SUDs. Next, you might conduct three or four imaginal prolonged-exposure exercises on your own, with these lasting a half hour or until your SUD dropped to four. Once your anxiety remained down, you might later conduct three or four prolonged-exposure exercises in real life: repeatedly driving across a bridge.

Basic Principles of Prolonged-Exposure Work

- Always preface prolonged-exposure work with brief-exposure work.

- Conduct prolonged-exposure work only after strong coping effects have developed by way of brief-exposure work.

- Understand the catastrophic or irrational appraisals embedded in the distress-inducing cues during prolonged-exposure work.

- Conduct imaginal prolonged-exposure work before conducting prolonged-exposure work in real life.

- Continue a prolonged-exposure exercise until the distress provoked at the outset of the exercise substantially subsides. At the conclusion, the distress should be about 50 percent of what it was at the outset. For example, if six SUDs are provoked at the beginning of an exercise, continue the exercise until there is a one-and-half-SUDs decrease to about four and a half. Remember, three SUDs are considered "normal" or "no distress."

- Use only rational thinking to manage distress during prolonged-exposure exercises. The eye-movement technique and the relaxation response should not be used until the 50-percent decrease in SUDs has occurred. This insures that the distraction and suppression processes inherent in these two emotion-focused coping skills do not inhibit the desensitization effect from developing.

- Terminate a prolonged-exposure exercise if it provokes an overwhelmingly intense level of distress, six and a half SUDs or more. Use the eye-movement technique and the relaxation response as well as rational thinking to do so. Afterward, a smaller subset of the distress-inducing cues should be selected for subsequent prolonged-exposure work, and/or additional brief-exposure work should be undertaken before resuming the prolonged-exposure work.

Relapse Prevention Work

Sessions 14 and 15

Goals:

- Complete a self-assessment to get an idea of how you are doing overall.

- Set the agenda by reviewing your treatment goals, your homework, your anxiety-disorder symptoms, and your life in general.

- Review the use of emotion-focused coping skills.

- Discuss relapse-prevention strategies.

- Terminate treatment.

- Negotiate homework assignments. Probable homework for this phase:

Continue to apply emotion-focused coping skills, problem-solve effectively, and don't fall back into old patterns of avoidance.

 The objective of this phase is to maintain the clinical gains that you have made. This is usually met by continuing to apply your newly acquired emotion-focused coping skills and by effectively problem-solving any situational stressors that arise. Controlling worry, keeping alcohol and other substances such as caffeine at a minimum, and maintaining good sleep habits are other ways to maintain the gains. Take care not to fall back into old habits of avoiding distressing situations. Should a relapse occur, do not assume that treatment failed. Instead, view it as an early wake-up call—you may need some additional exposure work on your own or with the assistance of your therapist.

 Now, as you approach the end of treatment, you are encouraged to retake the Modified Symptom Scale so you and your therapist can assess your progress.

Modified PTSD Symptom Scale

Developed by Sherry Falsetti, Heidi Resnick, Patricia Resick & Dean Kilpatrick
Medical University of South Carolina & University of Missouri—St. Louis

Instructions: The purpose of this scale is to measure the frequency and severity of symptoms in <u>the past two weeks</u>. Using the scale below, please indicate the frequency of symptoms to the left of each item. Then indicate the severity beside each item by circling the letter that fits you best.

FREQUENCY

0 = Not at all

1 = Once per week or less/a little bit/
   once in a while

2 = 2 to 4 times per week/somewhat/
   half the time

3 = 5 or more times per week/very much/
   almost

SEVERITY

A = Not at all distressing

B = A little bit distressing

C = Moderately distressing

D = Quite a bit distressing

E = Extremely distressing

FREQUENCY		SEVERITY
_____	1. Have you had recurrent or intrusive distressing thoughts or recollections about the event(s)?	A B C D E
_____	2. Have you been having recurrent bad dreams or nightmares about the event(s)?	A B C D E
_____	3. Have you had the experience of suddenly reliving the event(s), flashbacks of it, acting or feeling as if it were re-occurring?	A B C D E
_____	4. Have you been intensely emotionally upset when reminded of the event(s) (includes anniversary reactions)?	A B C D E
_____	5. Have you persistently been making efforts to avoid thoughts or feelings associated with the event(s) we've talked about?	A B C D E
_____	6. Have you persistently been making efforts to avoid activities, situations, or places that remind you of the event(s)?	A B C D E
_____	7. Are there any important aspects about the event(s) that you still cannot recall?	A B C D E
_____	8. Have you markedly lost interest in free time activities since the event(s)?	A B C D E

FREQUENCY

0 = Not at all

1 = Once per week or less/a little bit/ once in a while

2 = 2 to 4 times per week/somewhat/ half the time

3 = 5 or more times per week/very much/almost always

SEVERITY

A = Not at all distressing

B = A little bit distressing

C = Moderately distressing

D = Quite a bit distressing

E = Extremely distressing

FREQUENCY		SEVERITY
_____	9. Have you felt detached or cut off from others around you since the event(s)?	A B C D E
_____	10. Have you felt that your ability to experience emotions is less (e.g., unable to have loving feelings, feeling numb, can't cry when sad, etc.)?	A B C D E
_____	11. Have you felt that any future plans or hopes have changed because of the event(s) (e.g., no career, marriage, children, or long life)?	A B C D E
_____	12. Have you been having persistent difficulty falling or staying asleep?	A B C D E
_____	13. Have you been continuously irritable or having anger outbursts?	A B C D E
_____	14. Have you been having persistent difficulty concentrating?	A B C D E
_____	15. Are you overly alert (e.g., check to see who is around you) since the event(s)?	A B C D E
_____	16. Have you been jumpier, more easily startled, since the event(s)?	A B C D E
_____	17. Have you been having intense PHYSICAL REACTIONS (e.g., sweaty, heart palpitations) when reminded of the event(s)?	A B C D E

Program Satisfaction Questionnaire (PSQ)

Please evaluate the therapy program you have just completed by answering the following questions. Circle the number that best reflects your opinion. Your honest answer, whether positive or negative, will give us feedback to make the program better.

1. How effective was the therapy program in helping you with your problem?

1	2	3	4	5	6	7
Not effective		Moderately effective			Extremely effective	

2. How helpful were the homework and exercises in this therapy program?

1	2	3	4	5	6	7
Not helpful		Moderately helpful			Extremely helpful	

3. Were the skills you learned in this therapy program useful for coping with your problem?

1	2	3	4	5	6	7
Not useful		Moderately useful			Extremely useful	

4. Overall, how would you rate the quality of this therapy?

1	2	3	4	5	6	7
High quality		Moderate Quality			Low Quality	

5. If someone with a similar problem to yours asked for recommendations, how would you describe the usefulness of this therapy program?

1	2	3	4	5	6	7
Not useful		Moderately useful			Extremely useful	

6. If you could go back to remake your decision about this therapy program, would you do it again?

1	2	3	4	5	6	7
No definitely		Uncertain			Yes definitely	

7. How successfully were your goals met by this therapy program?

1	2	3	4	5	6	7
Goals met		Moderately successful with goals			Goals not met	

8. How would you rate your improvement in the symptoms that concerned you most?

1	2	3	4	5	6	7
Extremely improved		Moderately improved			Not improved	

Additional Reading

For More on PTSD:

Matsakis, A. 1998. *Trust after Trauma: A Guide to Relationships for Survivors and Those Who Love Them*. Oakland, Calif.: New Harbinger Publications.

———. *I Can't Get Over It: A Handbook for Trauma Survivors*. Oakland, Calif.: New Harbinger Publications, 1998.

———. 1991. *When the Bough Breaks: A Helping Guide for Parents of Sexually Abused Children*. Oakland, Calif.: New Harbinger Publications.

For More on Irrational Self-Talk:

Burns, David. 1980. *"Irrational" Self-Talk and Beliefs, the New Mood Therapy*. New York: Signet.

Ellis, Albert. 1975. *A New Guide to Rational Living*. Hollywood, Calif.: Prentice Hall.

McKay, M., M. Davis, and P. Fanning. 1998. *Thoughts & Feelings: Taking Control of Your Moods and Your Life*. Oakland, Calif.: New Harbinger Publications.

McKay, M., and P. Fanning. 1991. *Prisoners of Beliefs: Exposing and Changing Beliefs That Control Your Life*. Oakland, Calif.: New Harbinger Publications.

For More on Relaxation and Stress Management:

Benson, H. 1978. *The Relaxation Response*. New York: McGraw-Hill.

Davis, M., E. Eshelman, and M. McKay. 1995. *The Relaxation & Stress Reduction Workbook*. Oakland, Calif.: New Harbinger Publications.

Jacobson, E. 1978. *You Must Relax*. New York: McGraw-Hill.

Meichenbaum, D. 1985. *Stress Innoculation Training*. New York: Pergamon Press.

Suinn, R. 1990. *Anxiety Management Training*. New York: Plenum Press.

For More on Exercise:

Cooper, K. H. 1977. *The Aerobics Way*. New York: Bantam Books.

For More on Time Management:

Lakein, A. 1973. *How to Get Control of Your Time and Your Life*. New York: Peter Wyden.

McKenzie, R. A. 1975. *The Time Trap*. New York: McGraw-Hill.

Anxiety Disorders

For free brochures on any of the following disorders, send a stamped self-addressed envelope to:

American Psychiatric Association
Division of Public Affairs
Department SG
1400 K Street, N.W.
Washington, D.C. 20005

Anxiety disorders : ask for brochure #MDXA 2250; panic disorders: ask for brochure #MDXA 2262; phobias: ask for brochure #MDXA 2257; posttraumatic stress disorder: ask for brochure #MDXA 2258; obsessive-compulsive disorder: ask for brochure #MDXA 2256.

Some Other New Harbinger Self-Help Titles

Claiming Your Creative Self: True Stories from the Everyday Lives of Women, $15.95
Six Keys to Creating the Life You Desire, $19.95
Taking Control of TMJ, $13.95
What You Need to Know About Alzheimer's, $15.95
Winning Against Relapse: A Workbook of Action Plans for Recurring Health and Emotional Problems, $14.95
Facing 30: Women Talk About Constructing a Real Life and Other Scary Rites of Passage, $12.95
The Worry Control Workbook, $15.95
Wanting What You Have: A Self-Discovery Workbook, $18.95
When Perfect Isn't Good Enough: Strategies for Coping with Perfectionism, $13.95
The Endometriosis Survival Guide, $13.95
Earning Your Own Respect: A Handbook of Personal Responsibility, $12.95
High on Stress: A Woman's Guide to Optimizing the Stress in Her Life, $13.95
Infidelity: A Survival Guide, $13.95
Stop Walking on Eggshells, $14.95
Consumer's Guide to Psychiatric Drugs, $16.95
The Fibromyalgia Advocate: Getting the Support You Need to Cope with Fibromyalgia and Myofascial Pain, $18.95
Healing Fear: New Approaches to Overcoming Anxiety, $16.95
Working Anger: Preventing and Resolving Conflict on the Job, $12.95
Sex Smart: How Your Childhood Shaped Your Sexual Life and What to Do About It, $14.95
You Can Free Yourself From Alcohol & Drugs, $13.95
Amongst Ourselves: A Self-Help Guide to Living with Dissociative Identity Disorder, $14.95
Healthy Living with Diabetes, $13.95
Dr. Carl Robinson's Basic Baby Care, $10.95
Better Boundaries: Owning and Treasuring Your Life, $13.95
Goodbye Good Girl, $12.95
Being, Belonging, Doing, $10.95
Thoughts & Feelings, Second Edition, $18.95
Depression: How It Happens, How It's Healed, $14.95
Trust After Trauma, $15.95
The Chemotherapy & Radiation Survival Guide, Second Edition, $14.95
Surviving Childhood Cancer, $12.95
The Headache & Neck Pain Workbook, $14.95
Perimenopause, $16.95
The Self-Forgiveness Handbook, $12.95
A Woman's Guide to Overcoming Sexual Fear and Pain, $14.95
Don't Take It Personally, $12.95
Becoming a Wise Parent For Your Grown Child, $12.95
Clear Your Past, Change Your Future, $13.95
Preparing for Surgery, $17.95
The Power of Two, $15.95
It's Not OK Anymore, $13.95
The Daily Relaxer, $12.95
The Body Image Workbook, $17.95
Living with ADD, $17.95
When Anger Hurts Your Kids, $12.95
The Chronic Pain Control Workbook, Second Edition, $17.95
Fibromyalgia & Chronic Myofascial Pain Syndrome, $19.95
Kid Cooperation: How to Stop Yelling, Nagging & Pleading and Get Kids to Cooperate, $13.95
The Stop Smoking Workbook: Your Guide to Healthy Quitting, $17.95
Conquering Carpal Tunnel Syndrome and Other Repetitive Strain Injuries, $17.95
An End to Panic: Breakthrough Techniques for Overcoming Panic Disorder, Second Edition, $18.95
Letting Go of Anger: The 10 Most Common Anger Styles and What to Do About Them, $12.95
Messages: The Communication Skills Workbook, Second Edition, $15.95
Coping With Chronic Fatigue Syndrome: Nine Things You Can Do, $13.95
The Anxiety & Phobia Workbook, Second Edition, $18.95
The Relaxation & Stress Reduction Workbook, Fourth Edition, $17.95
Living Without Depression & Manic Depression: A Workbook for Maintaining Mood Stability, $18.95
Coping With Schizophrenia: A Guide For Families, $15.95
Visualization for Change, Second Edition, $15.95
Angry All the Time: An Emergency Guide to Anger Control, $12.95
Couple Skills: Making Your Relationship Work, $14.95
Self-Esteem, Second Edition, $13.95
I Can't Get Over It, A Handbook for Trauma Survivors, Second Edition, $16.95
Dying of Embarrassment: Help for Social Anxiety and Social Phobia, $13.95
The Depression Workbook: Living With Depression and Manic Depression, $17.95
Men & Grief: A Guide for Men Surviving the Death of a Loved One, $14.95
When Once Is Not Enough: Help for Obsessive Compulsives, $14.95
Beyond Grief: A Guide for Recovering from the Death of a Loved One, $14.95
Hypnosis for Change: A Manual of Proven Techniques, Third Edition, $15.95
When Anger Hurts, $13.95

Call **toll free, 1-800-748-6273,** to order. Have your Visa or Mastercard number ready. Or send a check for the titles you want to New Harbinger Publications, Inc., 5674 Shattuck Ave., Oakland, CA 94609. Include $3.80 for the first book and 75¢ for each additional book, to cover shipping and handling. (California residents please include appropriate sales tax.) Allow two to five weeks for delivery.

Prices subject to change without notice.